Exploring the Seasons

Exploring Fall

by Terri DeGezelle

CAPSTONE PRESS
a capstone imprint

Pebble Plus is published by Capstone Press,
1710 Roe Crest Drive, North Mankato, Minnesota 56003.
www.capstonepub.com

Library of Congress Cataloging-in-Publication Data
DeGezelle, Terri, 1955–
  Exploring fall / by Terri DeGezelle.
    p. cm. — (Pebble Plus. Exploring the seasons)
  Includes bibliographical references and index.
  Summary: "Color photos and simple text introduce the fall season"—Provided by publisher.
  ISBN 978-1-4296-7696-0 (library binding) — ISBN 978-1-4296-7908-4 (paperback)
  1. Autumn—Juvenile literature. I. Title. II. Series.
  QB637.7.D445 2012
  508.2—dc23   2011029889

Editorial Credits
Gillia Olson, editor; Sarah Bennett, designer; Svetlana Zhurkin, media researcher; Kathy McColley, production specialist

Photo Credits
Corbis: Royalty-free, 14–15, 20–21; Dreamstime: Tessarthetegu, 16–17; Image Ideas, 1; Photolibrary/Margaret Walton,
20 (inset); Shutterstock/Alexei Novikov, 5, Andrey Stepanov, 12–13, Elena Yakusheva, 18–19, Magdalena Bujak, cover
(center), Natali Glado, cover (right), silver-john, 10–11

Note to Parents and Teachers

The Exploring the Seasons series supports national science standards related to earth science.
This book describes and illustrates the fall season. The images support early readers in
understanding the text. The repetition of words and phrases helps early readers learn new
words. This book also introduces early readers to subject-specific vocabulary words, which are
defined in the Glossary section. Early readers may need assistance to read some words and to
use the Table of Contents, Glossary, Read More, Internet Sites, and Index sections of the book.

Printed in the United States of America in North Mankato, Minnesota.
102011   006405CGS12

Table of Contents

Season of Change

Fall is the season of change.

Everything gets ready for winter.

In the Northern Hemisphere,

the first day of fall, or autumn,

is September 22 or 23.

What Causes Seasons?

Earth travels around the sun

once a year on a tilted axis.

The tilt makes certain parts

of the planet point at the sun

at different times of the year.

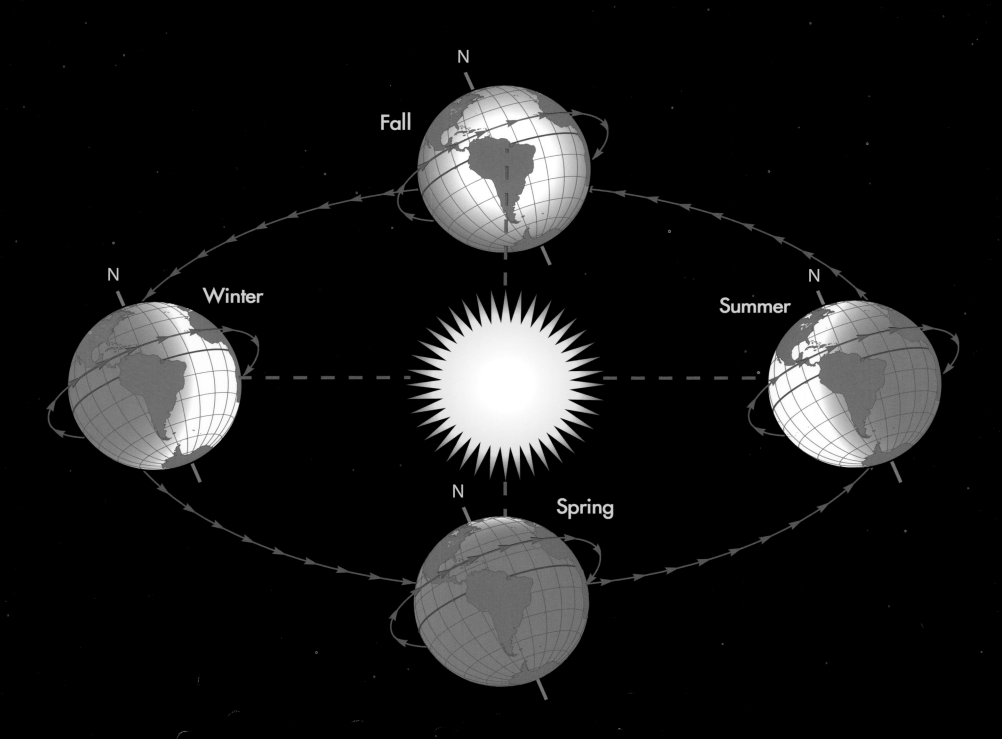

Fall

Winter

Summer

Spring

The seasons change as different parts of Earth point at the sun. Fall begins when Earth's axis starts to point away from the sun.

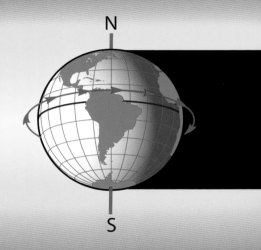

Daylight

Daylight gets shorter in fall.

The sun seems lower in the sky.

Less sunlight brings

lower temperatures.

Frost sometimes forms at night.

Water in Fall

Lakes and ponds get cold in fall. But oceans have built up warmth over the summer. The warm water makes hurricanes more common in fall.

Trees in Fall

In fall, trees get ready for winter.
Less light tells trees to stop
making food. Green leaves turn
yellow, red, or other colors.
Then the leaves fall off.

Animals in Fall

Animals get ready for winter too. Squirrels gather and store nuts. Bears gain weight to keep warm in winter. Some birds migrate to warmer places.

People in Fall

People dress for cool weather activities in fall. They wear long pants and sweaters. Football starts. People hike and bike before it gets cold.

North and South

Fall in the Northern Hemisphere is spring in the Southern Hemisphere. U.S. farmers harvest crops as Australian farmers plant crops.

Glossary

axis—a real or imaginary line through an object's center, around which the object turns

frost—a very thin layer of ice

harvest—to gather crops that are ripe

hemisphere—one half of Earth; the Northern and Southern hemispheres experience seasons opposite to each other

hurricane—a strong, swirling wind and rain storm that starts over the ocean

migrate—to move from one place to another for warmer weather or to find food

season—one of the four parts of the year; winter, spring, summer, and fall are seasons

temperature—how hot or cold something is

tilt—leaning; not straight

Read More

Bullard, Lisa. *Busy Animals: Learning about Animals in Autumn.* Autumn. Mankato, Minn.: Picture Window Books, 2011.

Rustad, Martha E. H. *Fall Leaves: Colorful and Crunchy.* Fall's Here! Minneapolis: Millbrook Press, 2011.

Smith, Sian. *Fall.* Seasons. Chicago: Heinemann Library, 2009.

Internet Sites

FactHound offers a safe, fun way to find Internet sites related to this book. All of the sites on FactHound have been researched by our staff.

Here's all you do:

Visit *www.facthound.com*

Type in this code: 9781429676960

 Check out projects, games and lots more at
www.capstonekids.com

Index

Word Count: 225

Grade: 1

Early-Intervention Level: 21